I0022079

IT Outsourcing Contracts

A Legal and Practical Guide

IT Outsourcing Contracts
A Legal and Practical Guide

JIMMY DESAI

IT Governance Publishing

Every possible effort has been made to ensure that the information contained in this book is accurate at the time of going to press, and the publishers and the author cannot accept responsibility for any errors or omissions, however caused. No responsibility for loss or damage occasioned to any person acting, or refraining from action, as a result of the material in this publication can be accepted by the publisher or the author.

Apart from any fair dealing for the purposes of research or private study, or criticism or review, as permitted under the Copyright, Designs and Patents Act 1988, this publication may only be reproduced, stored or transmitted, in any form, or by any means, with the prior permission in writing of the publisher or, in the case of reprographic reproduction, in accordance with the terms of licences issued by the Copyright Licensing Agency. Enquiries concerning reproduction outside those terms should be sent to the publishers at the following address:

IT Governance Publishing
IT Governance Limited
Unit 3, Clive Court
Bartholomew's
Walk Cambridgeshire Business Park
Ely
Cambridgeshire
CB7 4EH
United Kingdom
www.itgovernance.co.uk

© Jimmy Desai 2009

The author has asserted the rights of the author under the Copyright, Designs and Patents Act, 1988, to be identified as the author of this work.

First published in the United Kingdom in 2009
by IT Governance Publishing.

ISBN 978-1-84928-029-7

FOREWORD

This book has been written with the following readers in mind, although others should also find the information useful:

- Chief executive officers

- Managing directors

- Finance directors

- Strategic directors

- Senior management teams

- IT and outsourcing lawyers (both in private practice and in-house)

- Chief information officers and IT directors

- IT consultants

- IT managers

- IT procurement professionals

- IT sales professionals.

A wide range of industry sectors need IT and many organisations choose to outsource this (for example, banking, pharmaceuticals, travel and insurance companies). This can happen where an organisation outsources its IT payroll needs, its helpdesk and IT maintenance requirements, its payment processing or its whole IT function.

This book identifies some of the benefits and the pitfalls that an organisation can encounter when outsourcing its IT.

PREFACE

The idea for this book arose because numerous organisations were regularly encountering and seeking advice upon the same, or similar, legal and practical issues surrounding IT outsourcing.

Many of the issues that they were facing were not new. However, organisations were spending a lot of management time, effort and costs in deciphering the IT outsourcing equation and issues for themselves.

This time, effort and money could have been used to consider and solve more novel issues relating to IT outsourcing arrangements, rather than being spent on issues which were commonplace in the industry, and for which tried and tested solutions already existed.

The information in this book provides an overview of IT outsourcing, highlighting typical scenarios that can arise, and providing information on typical solutions that have been adopted by other organisations.

By providing a short, legal and practical guide to IT outsourcing, the reader should be able to quickly come up to speed with some of the legal and practical issues that might arise in an IT outsourcing contract.

ABOUT THE AUTHOR

Jimmy Desai is a partner at law firm Beachcroft LLP, in the City of London, and has been advising upon, formulating and implementing SLA contracts and strategies, benefits and cost savings for businesses, since the mid 1990s. Throughout his career he has advised major international blue-chip companies, governments, industry bodies, IT customers and suppliers on their service level agreements.

He writes extensively for a wide range of IT publications, and lectures at international conferences, both in the UK and abroad. He has lectured at the University of London and the University of Stirling and, as well as a law degree, he has a Masters Degree (First Class) in Electronic Engineering and postgraduate qualifications in Intellectual Property Law and Practice.

Jimmy is a member of TIPLO (The Intellectual Property Lawyers Organisation), ITMA (The Institute of Trade Mark Agents), SCL (The Society for Computers and Law), EuroITcounsel, Intellect (an IT trade body), and ITechLaw.

Jimmy is listed as one of the top 40 Internet and e-commerce lawyers in the UK in the International Who's Who of Internet and E-Commerce Lawyers 2010.

ACKNOWLEDGEMENTS

This is my first book for IT Governance Ltd. and has been written whilst working as a lawyer in the City of London, where I advise numerous clients on their legal needs and strategies in obtaining better services at lower costs, to make their businesses more successful.

It could not have been written without the support and assistance of my colleagues; a very understanding and patient publisher in the form of Angela Wilde at IT Governance Ltd, and the support of friends, family and clients when talking about the ideas and principles involved in this book.

I am also grateful for the patience, support and input of my wife, Sarah Hanchet, without whom this book would not have been possible.

CONTENTS

INTRODUCTION

This book provides an overview of the IT outsourcing relationship and life cycle. It is written from the perspective of the customer, and so references to 'you', 'your', 'your organisation', 'the organisation' or 'an organisation', are references to the customer.

The IT outsourcing process often begins with an organisation considering whether or not IT outsourcing would be of benefit (e.g. outsourcing its payroll systems, certain IT functions or its whole IT department), and then the issues which would need to be considered in order to answer this question accurately, are discussed.

If an organisation believes that an IT outsourcing deal could be of benefit, it will then need to choose a suitable supplier. The issues to consider are also set out in this book.

Having selected an IT supplier, an organisation will then need to agree key terms (including identifying and agreeing any contentious issues which are so-called deal breakers), to avoid disputes or business disruption later on.

Agreeing the IT outsourcing contract is not the end, but the start, of the IT outsourcing relationship, and this relationship will need to be managed and developed over the course of the contract. Sooner or later, the IT outsourcing arrangement will have to come to an end and so an exit plan will need to be formulated and implemented.

This life cycle needs to be fully understood by anyone involved in this kind of IT outsourcing transaction, and this book provides useful information about the life cycle.

CHAPTER 1: WHY DO ORGANISATIONS CONSIDER IT OUTSOURCING?

IT outsourcing can provide many benefits for your organisation, including cost savings and improved services.

If you outsource your IT to a third party (e.g. by outsourcing your payroll systems, certain IT functions or your whole IT department), the arrangement between you will take the form of a legally enforceable contract (which will include a service level agreement). The IT outsourcing contract is the umbilical cord between you and your IT supplier in respect of your IT system requirements.

Therefore, it is vital that your IT outsourcing contract is drafted properly, so that it caters for all of your requirements. This is because you – as the customer – are likely to become heavily dependent upon the arrangements with your IT supplier, and changes later on to what you want them to do, are likely to lead to extra costs and possible delays for your day-to-day business.

Furthermore, ending an IT outsourcing contract can be problematic, if the arrangements governing the end of the contract are not clear, including arrangements for potentially ending the contract early. Because your organisation is likely to have become dependent on your outsourced IT arrangements, you need to ensure – as part of the outsourcing contract – that there will be a smooth transition back to your own in-house department, or to a replacement IT supplier that you have nominated, in order to avoid business disruption.

Choosing to outsource your IT

Choosing whether or not to outsource your IT is a strategic business decision that can be made for quality and/or financial reasons. There are lots of definitions of IT outsourcing, the most usual being:

'Taking internal company functions, and paying an outside organisation to handle them.' This is often called 'contracting out'. Outsourcing is done to save money, improve quality, or free up company resources for other activities.

'The subcontracting of activities (production, processes or services), that are not regarded as part of a company's core business.' This means delegating non-core operations, or jobs from internal production, to an external entity (such as a subcontractor) that specialises in that operation.

A subset of the term (offshoring) involves transferring jobs to another country, either by hiring local subcontractors, or building a facility in an area where labour is cheap.

It is worth reflecting here on the IT industry view of offshoring. In March 2009, it was reported that JP Morgan would increase its outsourcing to India by 25%, to nearly US$400 million, from present levels of US$250-300 million. JP Morgan's chief information officer is also quoted as saying that the organisation will increase outsourcing to India. Opinions in early 2009 have tended to suggest that India will remain a top outsourcing destination because it has a technically and English-proficient urban workforce, whose wages are much lower than those of their Western counterparts.

It is also worth noting here the issue of business focus. The perceived wisdom has been that if a business specialises in a certain sector (e.g. financial services), then that business should devote its entire staff, time, effort and resources to that 'core business' (e.g. financial services) rather than towards its IT needs. Indeed, as many organisations' core business has grown, they have found that they need a simpler and more cost-effective means of obtaining IT, without having to manage and fund a complex IT department.

However, there have been cases where organisations have initially outsourced their IT requirements to third parties, only to later bring it back in-house. The main reason for this has been that the organisation's IT is seen to be so critical to the business, that it was felt to be too much of a risk to rely on a third party IT supplier.

Therefore, although many organisations outsource their IT function in order to save money, gain greater control and buy in greater expertise, this is not without its risks. You will want to consider what the best option is for you, depending on the business you are in, and how close you feel you need to be to the IT support in your organisation.

In summary, if you are considering outsourcing your IT, you will need to decide whether someone else might be able to provide this function for you more efficiently; and also whether IT is 'core' to your organisation's business or a support function. The next section considers some of the advantages and disadvantages of IT outsourcing.

Advantages of IT outsourcing

IT outsourcing can enable your organisation to operate more efficiently, and potentially make more profit. The main considerations for many organisations are outlined below.

Cost savings

Cost savings can include:

Staff costs: If an organisation does not employ its own IT staff then it can save staff wages as well as other staff costs, including National Insurance payments, sickness and holiday pay, bonuses, pensions and other staff benefits (memberships, travel allowances, training costs, etc).

An organisation can also save the time, cost and resources necessary to manage and organise its own IT staff (e.g. management and HR).

The IT supplier's staff are also often on lower wages, particularly if they are based in countries such as India, South Africa or the Far East. These costs savings can be passed through by the IT supplier to your organisation.

Your organisation may also welcome the relative simplicity of paying an IT supplier an agreed fee each month, so that you can budget for your IT spend (and avoid various hidden costs – such as unplanned overtime, pensions, sick pay, maternity pay – which may exist if IT is provided internally).

Premises and related costs: Premises and all of the office equipment and resources that are necessary for your own IT department, may no longer be needed (e.g. office furniture, office computers and IT systems).

Equipment costs: If the IT supplier is responsible for keeping IT equipment and software up to date, then all upgrades, modifications and fixes are provided without your organisation having to own and pay for all of this.

IT equipment and software may be licensed to your organisation by the IT supplier, which avoids you having to pay for it up front and/or find space to house it. This will also mean that you won't suffer from depreciation in the price of such equipment.

In addition, IT suppliers can obtain IT equipment and software at a bulk discount which might not be available to your organisation. This is one of the key ways in which IT suppliers offer a more cost-effective service than many companies can achieve in house.

Ensuring a better service

Often organisations running their own IT department will not specifically define what service is to be provided to support their core business. As a consequence, they will not monitor the performance of their own internal department. Without knowing the standard of service or the response times they are receiving from their internal IT department, it is difficult to identify the scope for potential efficiency gains. In the event of an organisation's IT department not providing a good service, there may be an attempt to 'performance manage' the IT team. However, in the end there may be no other option but to try and replace people. This all takes time and effort, and costs the organisation money in terms of dismissing, replacing and/or recruiting IT staff, and can divert attention away from strategic objectives.

Many organisations decide, instead, to outsource their IT function, because they can more easily define and control the

IT services which an IT supplier can provide and this frees up resources.

An organisation that outsources its IT function can also specify exactly the kind of service it would like, the standards required, and how the service will be provided.

Furthermore, the IT outsourcing contract can stipulate the services which you do not require or do not need (and do not want to pay for), which ensures that you are in charge of defining your IT requirements. This is important for two reasons. Firstly, in respect of day-to-day business, many organisations find that they do not have the time or expertise to closely manage the work of their in-house IT team. This can mean that in-house staff start to pursue their own IT interests, rather than those of the chief executive officer.

It might also be that where your organisation needs to expand its operations, a 'step change' is required in IT support. This level of internal investment might not be as focused (and therefore cost-effective) as outsourcing to a third party, which is likely to offer cost savings via greater expertise and economies of scale.

Advantages of IT outsourcing are sometimes ignored, or not considered, by organisations where the internally provided IT services are seen as 'good enough'. However, there are some organisations that are concerned about whether or not IT is being managed in the most efficient, cost-effective and streamlined way, and whether or not its IT function and IT employees are fully aligned with the objectives of the organisation as a whole.

Engaging an IT supplier

Engaging an IT supplier can help you to define, monitor and understand your IT systems and IT needs more fully.

Monitor the service – You can check at regular intervals that you are obtaining the services which you have paid for, and that the standard of those services is in line with your contract.

External expertise – You can benefit from the IT supplier's external expertise, as they are likely to be working for a portfolio of customers and have up-to-date skills and know-how. These skills are likely to be more advanced, sophisticated and/or holistic compared to that of your own IT department, especially since the IT supplier's staff may generally be more experienced, having dealt with a large number of customer accounts.

Compensation – If your organisation does not receive the service that you have paid for; and/or if the services are not provided to pre-agreed standards, you are likely to be entitled to service credits. These are pre-agreed, fixed amounts of money which are paid to you as the customer for any defaults by the IT supplier in the service provided. Furthermore, the service agreement should also entitle you to seek compensation for poor standards of service, if this should amount to a breach of contract. If you receive poor service from your own in-house IT department, such compensation would not be available.

Flexibility – If you have your own fully-staffed IT department, then regardless of how your organisation's IT needs change, you will still have to pay your staff. In particular, if your organisation does not need all of its IT staff all of the time, or perhaps needs them on an *ad hoc* 'call in' basis, then you will still have to pay for them on a fulltime basis.

Outsourcing IT can therefore provide your organisation with flexibility, as you only pay for the IT which you need. Under this sort of arrangement, you can also 'flex' your IT requirements (by either reducing or increasing them, or by adding completely different IT goods or services to the package which you originally contracted for). The terms upon which changes can occur will be set out in the IT outsourcing contract, which is why – coming back to where we started – this contract is of vital importance.

An important first step in keeping costs down is to choose your IT supplier (perhaps from a list of possible contenders) using clear criteria. This will ensure that when the time comes to 'do a deal', you will have ensured that you are negotiating with a supplier that can provide what you need and is also in your price bracket.

That said, although IT outsourcing brings many benefits, there are major issues which cannot be ignored and will need to be addressed before an IT outsourcing deal is completed. Giving consideration to these issues at a very early stage will help you negotiate a clearer deal which in turn will ensure that you are not faced with unexpected costs.

Disadvantages of IT outsourcing

Lower cost savings than anticipated

Unexpected costs can eat into projected cost savings, so much so that an organisation can, in some cases, end up losing money by outsourcing its IT. These costs can arise in a variety of ways:

Deal costs

These can escalate dramatically. The cost of consultants, legal advisers and accountants, in relation to negotiating, documenting and finalising a deal, can all add significantly to the costs. This is particularly the case if the deal is of high value, is offshore (i.e. where foreign advisers are also required), and takes many months (if not years) to complete.

Doing deals in foreign jurisdictions can, in some cases, require the approval of third parties (e.g. government departments or regulatory bodies), and this can lead to unexpected delays, extra fees, and/or extra work may need to be carried out by the organisation and its advisers to obtain the relevant approvals or permissions. These can all add to the cost of the deal.

Staff costs

The existing IT department may need to be made redundant or transferred to the IT supplier. In any event, this is likely to add to the costs.

The staff costs of offshore workers, and their mobility between different offshore providers (as such offshore workers look for better remuneration and better jobs at different offshore IT suppliers), can mean that the potential staff cost saving in using offshore workers as part of an IT outsourcing deal, may not be as great as originally anticipated.

Premises

If your organisation does not need as many IT staff, then it may not need the premises which house those IT staff. Hence, it may need to break leases for premises which may cost your organisation more than if such leases were allowed to expire in the normal way.

Redundant IT equipment

If your organisation outsources its IT requirements to a third party, then it might be left with old and redundant IT equipment which it simply has no need for. Therefore, the cost of this will have to be written off, and/or such equipment disposed of. An organisation may also have to pay for replacement equipment (either by buying new equipment, or leasing or licensing such equipment from the IT supplier).

Cancelling existing contracts

If an organisation chooses to outsource its IT to a single supplier, then all of its existing contracts (for example, any IT support or maintenance contracts, any equipment leasing contracts), will need to be cancelled or transferred to the new IT supplier. This may cost the organisation more than originally anticipated (for example, early termination costs regarding termination of any existing contracts).

Regulation

Some organisations are governed by regulatory regimes which require them to abide by certain rules and regulations. For example, banks will need to consider the Financial Services and Markets Act 2000 (FSMA) and The European Parliament and Council Directive and Markets in Financial Instruments (No. 2004/39/EC) (MIFID). They will also need to ensure that their IT systems are robust and secure. If an organisation is subject to regulatory regimes, it will need to ensure that its preferred IT supplier complies with such regimes. This could mean that the IT supplier has to do extra work and/or provide additional services, which in turn could raise costs (particularly if the IT outsourcing is going to be offshore).

Contract management

Some organisations may believe that the contract with the IT supplier will 'run itself', with no real input from themselves. However, this is often not the case. More usually, organisations will need to employ IT or project management staff to manage the IT outsourcing contract on a daily, weekly and monthly basis. This will ensure that organisations continue to obtain the services they have contracted for. Internal staff costs related to managing the outsourced contract, therefore, need to be factored into any IT outsourcing business arrangement.

Public relations

If an organisation closes down its internal IT department and outsources to an IT supplier, it could lead to negative press. For example, if IT is offshored to places such as India or the Far East, the press and public perception may be of job losses in the UK. Hence, an organisation (particularly if it is a household name) may incur significant public relations and marketing costs in explaining the position and business rationale for IT outsourcing, in order to protect its brand and reputation.

Additional purchases

The IT supplier will naturally want to sell more goods and/or services to your organisation throughout the term of the IT outsourcing contract, and may put significant marketing efforts into doing so.

Extra goods and/or services might include new equipment, software, updates, upgrades and/or modifications to existing equipment or software. In any event, if an organisation purchases extra goods and/or services during the IT outsourcing contract, then this will cost more than what might have originally been budgeted for at the outset. Again, the costs of any additional purchases should be factored in to any business case that an organisation prepares in relation to IT outsourcing.

Hidden costs

Your organisation could be charged for, or have to bear, the costs of a multitude of other goods and services relating to the IT outsourcing contract, including:

*   Changes to the goods and/or services which were originally contracted for (no matter how minor the change is to these).

*   Requests for additional goods or services which were not pre-agreed (but which are absolutely essential for the customer to obtain the benefit of the services provided).

*   Price increases and reviews on a regular basis.

*   The IT supplier developing and implementing exit plans or disaster recovery plans. Exit plans may arise such that on termination or expiry of the contract, the IT supplier may then reserve the right to charge extra for assisting your organisation, in relation to either transferring the IT systems back to you or to a replacement IT supplier that has been chosen by your organisation.

*   The costs of obtaining legal advice and/or taking any legal action if things do not go to plan.

*   The costs of obtaining a replacement IT supplier or re-establishing your own IT department at the end of the contract.

These 'hidden costs' may not be discretionary, in that your organisation may have no option but to pay them, because you are either bound to do so in the IT outsourcing contract (e.g. if you have agreed to upward only annual price reviews), or cannot operate your business properly without certain changes being made to the IT services.

Summary

Many organisations do not have enough information about their in-house IT department to know whether it is the most cost-effective way of providing IT support.

Organisations that benchmark their in-house functions, find that outsourcing their IT support provides cost savings and offers greater flexibility in the face of business changes.

There are both advantages and disadvantages to IT outsourcing. The main disadvantages concern escalating costs which arise because the organisation has not done enough preparation prior to starting contract negotiations. Therefore, before you even consider entering into negotiations with an IT supplier for an IT outsourcing deal, you will need to consider all of the factors above, to see whether or not you can really benefit from IT outsourcing.

Finally, if an organisation does decide to outsource its IT function to a third party, then the IT outsourcing contract (including the service level agreement), is vital to the efficiency and smooth running of the arrangement.

CHAPTER 2: HOW TO CHOOSE AN IT OUTSOURCING SUPPLIER

Having decided to outsource your organisation's IT function (all, or part of it), you now need to find a supplier. There are many such companies in the market, and they all have unique selling points, so you may find it difficult to decide straightaway which one to choose.

Most organisations facing this situation have reaped the benefits of careful selection planning. It is not always the case that the biggest global named IT supplier, or the cheapest, will be the right one for your company's needs.

A typical selection process

The process usually follows various steps, typically (but not always) following a route which involves the following.

An organisation will normally develop and finalise a specification which it would like implemented by a new supplier. It will then go on to ask various IT suppliers for a proposal. This proposal will be for the provision of IT goods and services in line with the broad specification.

Organisations usually state in their specification that they want a similar (or improved) service to the one that they were receiving from their internal IT department. However, since (as discussed in Chapter 1) few organisations have ever fully and completely defined the service provided by their internal IT department, and even fewer are able to describe the standards of such service, in most cases this is a rather broad definition.

The danger with an organisation only having a vague idea of IT goods and services required (as opposed to a clear defined specification at the outset), is that it can lose track of what it actually wanted in the first place. It can then end up being attracted to and buying IT goods and/or services which it may not really need. This can then mean spending far more money than was ever originally envisaged. Hence, time spent by organisations in developing a clear specification at the outset (together with a defined budget), will certainly help purchasing decisions later on in the process.

IT suppliers will often have a fixed menu of goods and services with set prices. However, this menu will rarely describe exactly what the customer wants. Therefore, the next stage is usually when the customer asks for amended or updated proposals from the IT suppliers, with more information that is tailored to its needs.

Each selected IT supplier then normally provides an amended offer, and an organisation will look at these and choose the one which most closely meets its requirements (in terms of cost, services, standards, etc).

Unless an organisation has spent considerable time in drawing up a clear and complete specification of its needs before getting into this process, it may well be that the offering it chooses is not very close to what it originally wanted.

However, many organisations enter into this process without this clearly defined specification and budget and, therefore often end up purchasing more, and/or different IT goods and services, at a much greater cost than was originally envisaged.

Potential dispute areas

Having selected a supplier, things should now run smoothly, with the supplier providing goods and services according to what has been agreed. However, problems often arise, and these can result in disputes and some even lead to litigation through the courts.

In many cases, problems arise because an organisation has not chosen IT goods and services that fit its business needs. It is essential that the customer chooses IT services which fit with its exact day-to-day needs, its culture (way of doing business), and overall business and strategic goals. It is therefore important that your organisation does not choose IT services solely on the basis of price, the brand name of the IT supplier, personal contacts, or other reasons which are not directly relevant to the business objectives behind outsourcing the IT function.

The following is a typical scenario that comes up again and again between organisations and suppliers, especially in the early days of a contract.

In negotiations, an organisation can easily be seduced by an IT supplier (often during discussions about the service contract) into ordering something which it did not originally think it required, or did not know existed because it is told that this is business critical. For example, this can happen if the organisation is told that it can have some leading-edge technology which is better and more advanced than others have. Thereby, making the organisation somehow more advanced and sophisticated (although the organisation may not fully appreciate that this may not be as tried and tested as more standard technology, and they could fare just as well with standard technology which many others use).

The next step towards a dispute arising is if the organisation realises after contract signature that it has purchased goods and/or services that do not particularly fit with what it needs. It may try to change its requirements, to be told by the IT supplier that this will take extra time and will cost more.

The organisation at this point is tied into, and heavily dependent upon, the IT supplier, and therefore cannot exit (or can exit, but with unacceptable disruption or cost implications). A typical cause of this problem is that the organisation may not have known what it wanted in the first place, or was not clear exactly how much it wanted to spend over the lifetime of the IT contract, or how costs might escalate and rise over time.

The organisation may then find that it is not able to afford the amended goods and services required, and/or cannot operate its business properly without them.

Litigation can ensue, as the organisation tries to exit the contract if at all possible under its terms (and try to find a cheaper alternative). The organisation may argue that it is somehow not obtaining the services which it wanted (such that there has been a material breach of the contract or some other

IT supplier default), in order to exit the contract and again try to find a cheaper alternative; or may demand the amended services from the IT supplier, but on the basis of the original price agreed for the original IT goods and services.

It is, of course, possible to avoid these problems. The next section explains how.

Mistakes to avoid when selecting your IT supplier

Size of IT supplier

As we have highlighted, a common mistake is to choose your IT supplier based on a brand name; for example, going with a global IT supplier based on name alone, regardless of your own organisation's size, location, budget, way of working or business requirements.

Large global IT suppliers typically supply large global organisations, and small organisations might find that they are not given the service or attention that they were expecting. This might be because the large IT supplier has many other customers who shout louder (and pay more), and your smaller organisation might not be regarded as being as important as the larger customers.

Smaller organisations may also find it difficult to have much of a voice with a large (global) IT supplier. During service agreement discussions, and if service levels give cause for concern, the global IT supplier will have the resources, legal department and financial backing to dictate terms, both at the contract negotiation stage and throughout the contract term.

The corollary is choosing an IT supplier that is much smaller than your own organisation.

The smaller IT supplier might not be able to cater for all of your requirements for a number of reasons which could include:

• The smaller IT supplier might have a number of customer accounts (both initially and/or after the deal is signed) which they then struggle to service properly, due to a lack of staff and resources, which can only be addressed via a step change in size.

- The smaller IT supplier might not be large enough to obtain bulk discount savings. Although this may not matter if you are a sole trader or a very small company, these lost savings could be significant for an organisation of even a medium size.

- If your organisation grows, the IT supplier may not be able to provide the additional IT goods and/or services that are required to keep pace with your needs.

- The IT supplier might not have the financial resources to make good any problems that could arise (by either dedicating extra staff to resolving the issue, or by promptly compensating you for lost business).

- The small IT supplier may be more likely to experience financial difficulties in difficult economic times; in which case this could have an impact upon the IT services it provides to your organisation.

However, all is not lost! The two scenarios above regarding choice of IT supplier, are not automatically fatal, and, remember, many organisations find themselves in one or other of these situations (going with a global supplier or a supplier that is too small to keep pace). With a properly considered and well-drafted IT outsourcing contract, things can work out perfectly well with both a larger global IT supplier or a small one, but extra caution needs to be exercised by all parties if the scenarios above are to be avoided.

That said, it is worth noting that a good match often occurs where the customer and IT supplier are of an equivalent size and with generally equal bargaining positions. This means that the outcome of any contract negotiations is likely to be fairly balanced. Furthermore, in practice, your organisation is likely to have the services provided to a sufficient standard and is likely to be treated as a reasonably important account of the IT supplier (such that the IT supplier is willing to listen to your organisation's concerns and act promptly to address issues which arise).

Public sector process[1]

It is worth pointing out that where governments, public bodies or other government-related bodies are selecting IT suppliers, then they tend to follow a detailed process of selection. Procurement rules and regulations mean that IT suppliers in this sort of situation will have to go through a set tendering process. This is useful for an organisation in two ways. Firstly, there will often be a reasonably clear and complete service specification, which is circulated with an opportunity for suppliers to ask detailed questions; and secondly, it must be shown that the IT supplier selection process was transparent and fair against a set of criteria. describing what the organisation was looking for, and that the organisation obtained value for money.

Although this sort of process is usually considered too onerous for most small to medium-sized organisations in the private sector, there is certainly value in being clear from the outset what are your requirements and bottom lines.

The next section goes on to consider a further area where disputes commonly arise.

Getting pricing right

Sometimes contracts do not contain all of the pricing information or the exact dates of payment but rely instead on either formulas or explanations about how much and when payments are due.

The difficulty with this approach is that the formulas and descriptions can be open to interpretation and if large sums (in the hundreds of thousands or tens of millions of pounds) are involved. then disputes can arise as to how much is due (if anything), and when exactly payments are due.

To avoid this type of argument, it is strongly recommended that IT outsourcing contracts:

---

[1] See *www.certes.co.uk/catalist/* where information is provided about the process used by government bodies in selecting IT suppliers.

- Clearly state when payments are due (in advance or in arrears).

- Clearly state if any interest is payable on overdue payments.

- Ensure that exact prices are set out in a schedule, together with the currency of payment (e.g. £ or US$), and who bears the risk for any currency fluctuations.

- Ensure that the dates for payment, and amounts due, are set out in a table, so that it is clear how much is due, when it is due and what the payment is for.[2]

- Clearly explain any price increases that may take place. It is common to find reference to annual price reviews (usually upwards!), but the contract should clarify that such reviews should be capped annually at, say, the level of the retail price index, or some other index, or at a fixed percentage.

If there is some variance as to how much might be due at any particular time, such that a formula is used, then worked examples should be included to show how this formula will operate in practice. Preparing worked examples also assists in flushing out any discrepancies which might arise.

From your organisation's point of view, the IT outsourcing contract needs to include the following sorts of payment provisions, and all or some payments should be linked to certain milestones or deliverables being achieved and delivered to your satisfaction.

Payment in arrears

This is the ability to withhold payments (or a certain percentage of payments), if services are not provided, or if they are not provided to the correct standards.

---

[2] In the Fujitsu v EDS case, major litigation arose as to whether or not a particular cost had been incorporated into agreements between the parties, and whether or not such a cost was payable.

Most favoured nation clauses

Asking for this type of clause, means that you are trying to ensure that your organisation is not paying any more for its IT services than any of the IT supplier's other customers at the time of the contract and/or in the future; and that, if any discounts or special deals are offered by the IT supplier to its other customers at any time, then these will also be offered to you at the same time. This kind of clause is often hotly contested by the IT supplier for various reasons, including that this deal is bespoke for your organisation. However, your organisation may raise this since, even if it does not get everything that it might want here, by conceding aspects on this clause, it may give itself the opportunity to ask for and obtain concessions from the IT supplier in other parts of the IT outsourcing contract.

Breakdown of costs

It is useful to have a thorough breakdown of where all costs will be incurred, in order to 'flush out' any hidden costs for which your organisation may subsequently be liable. For example, if your organisation purchases goods and/or services from an IT supplier, are these dependent upon the goods and/or services of other third parties (i.e. will you need additional equipment or software from other parties in order to operate the IT supplier's goods and services) and, if so, how much will this cost?

Reducing IT services

Here, you can try to obtain an option in the IT outsourcing contract, to reduce the IT services required (but not usually to less than a certain minimum or floor), and thereby may pay less overall for the contract than agreed.

Benchmarking

This is where your organisation can compare and contrast the IT supplier's services and associated costs against market norms at fixed periods of time (for example, every two years), and ask for reductions in prices if they are higher than IT market norms. A problem here is that the IT supplier may say that your organisation's goods and services are bespoke, and therefore difficult to compare on a like for like basis with standard market products. Nevertheless, there are formulas (including adjustments) which can be used to benchmark, in order to ensure that your organisation is not paying more for IT goods and services than it should be. Benchmarking is particularly useful in a long-term contract if prices are initially low but rise rapidly. If benchmarking is introduced, then ask for downward price adjustments only, otherwise you could pay more after the benchmarking exercise!

Open-book accounting from the IT supplier

This is where the IT supplier offers the customer visibility and transparency about how much the goods and services are actually costing them to provide; and how much they are actually charging the customer for these.

IT suppliers tend not to want open-book accounting because, amongst other things, it shows your organisation how much profit is being made by the IT supplier, and they may want to keep this confidential.

However, some IT suppliers (particularly small or medium-sized ones) may, in certain cases, provide open-book accounting to organisations (particularly if this will win tenders in a competitive situation with larger organisations).

Larger organisations might feel more comfortable contracting with smaller IT suppliers if there is open-book accounting. This is because it allows an organisation to operate as if the IT supplier were the organisation's own internal IT department, since they have complete access to information about the cost, operation and structure of the IT services provided. Overall, this way of working can serve to build trust.

Negotiating price and payment terms

When negotiating price and payment terms, your organisation can often expect the IT supplier to have its own thoughts on this which it will often say are standard, or part of company policy. However, often these clauses are subject to negotiation (particularly if the IT supplier needs your organisation's business). IT suppliers may want to secure orders during certain parts of the year where they are measuring revenues, such as the end of its financial half year or end of year. They will be keen to post the best figures that they can to impress their investors and shareholders. Typically, the IT supplier may ask for:

- Clauses to explain that the customer has only a certain amount of time to dispute invoices (after which they will be deemed to have been accepted and will be paid).

- Clauses to explain that the customer is obliged to pay any undisputed portions of invoices (even if the whole invoice is disputed).

- The ability to suspend the provision of IT goods and services if invoices are not paid (until such time as these invoices are paid).

- A change control mechanism, such that if goods or services are provided which are not 'in scope' (i.e. within the goods and services agreed in the IT outsourcing contract), then the IT supplier can charge more for these extra goods and services.

- Upward only uncapped price reviews at regular intervals (i.e. annually).

- The ability to charge interest on late payments (typically at a rate which is a few percentage points above the base rate of the IT supplier's bank).

However, do not drive such a hard bargain that your deal is one of the IT supplier's least profitable. Otherwise, the IT supplier can become de-motivated, or it can concentrate on other, more lucrative, contracts which could result in your organisation receiving a poor service.

So far we have considered how many organisations go about choosing an IT supplier, the potential bear-traps, and the importance of a robust IT outsourcing contract to regulate the power relationships between the parties. We have gone on to look at one key aspect of such a contract – price. This next section looks in a little more detail at some of the other selection criteria that you might like to consider as you think about choosing an IT supplier to run all, or some, of your IT functions.

Making the right choice of IT supplier – other selection criteria

Further issues that you should normally consider when choosing an IT supplier include:

- Understanding your organisation's IT needs (both now and in the future), and being able to explain these to an IT supplier in a clear and coherent way.

- Using independent consultants and other advisers (e.g. specialist IT outsourcing lawyers and accountants) to assess potential IT suppliers and any responses which they provide, in respect of what is best for your business.

- Asking IT suppliers for references and visiting reference sites where they are conducting work for organisations of a similar size and nature to your organisation.

- Speaking with existing customers of the IT supplier, and asking about the service provided by them (together trying to cater for any problems that they have encountered in their IT outsourcing contract with the IT supplier).

- Assessing whether the IT supplier understands, and caters for, your particular industry sector. Does the IT supplier work for other organisations which are in your industry? This can be useful, so you don't have to waste time (at your cost!) educating them as to how your industry sector works and why you need certain IT goods and services to operate in a certain way.

- Seeing any IT supplier's contractual documentation as early as possible to spot potential contentious issues, or difficult clauses, early on. If there are certain clauses which are completely unacceptable to you, or which your advisers say should be unacceptable (clauses which are so called 'show stoppers' or 'deal breakers'), then it is better to talk about these at the very start. If a compromise, or workaround, cannot be achieved at the start of talks, then there may be no point in spending time, effort and costs talking about the deal any further.

•   Using soft data (meetings, discussions, etc.) to make a 'gut feel' assessment of whether or not the IT supplier will fit in with your organisation's culture and way of working. For example, are you very organised and good at planning? Or do you take a deadline to the wire? This will affect how you expect your IT supplier to respond to you.

However, remember that the people that you are talking with about the IT outsourcing contract (salespeople, business development personnel and sales negotiators) are unlikely to be fully involved in implementing the contract in the years to come. Therefore, although you may like certain personnel at the IT supplier, it is, in fact, the terms of the IT outsourcing contract which will prevail. There is no guarantee that the staff you deal with, will be dealing with you for the duration of the contract (and, in all likelihood, you will be dealing with other staff who, in the case of potential disputes, will quote the terms of the IT outsourcing contract to you, regardless of verbal assurances that may have been given to you by the IT supplier's sales personnel).

Try to make an assessment of the extent to which the IT supplier understands, and will cater for, your organisation's needs, in respect of being flexible in providing goods and/or services. Is your business about to make a step change in size? Are you moving into areas that require different sorts of IT support? You may wish to test out how an IT supplier has responded to these business changes with other customers.

Try to make an assessment of the IT supplier's technological expertise, technical support and its ability to successfully solve customer IT problems. This can feel quite daunting. Some organisations pay for external advice from the IT supplier sector. Others take real-life problems and ask the IT supplier to describe how they would solve them in business terms.

However you assess the suitability of the IT supplier for your organisation, you need to ask the right questions and digest, understand and absorb the answers that are given, using specialists, such as IT outsourcing lawyers, to help you interpret what exactly the IT supplier is proposing.

Summary

Ideally, your relationship with your IT supplier should be a working partnership, based on a complete definition of your business needs and ways of working, and a clear definition of what both parties can expect from each other.

Some organisations choose their IT supplier for potentially the wrong reasons, and end up over the contract duration in an uneven or uncomfortable power relationship, or unable to get the support they need. In this case, whereas the IT supplier was brought in to solve the organisation's problems, it then can become one of the organisation's biggest problems.

It is not easy to make the right choice. There are a lot of IT suppliers in the market, and there is rarely enough time to do all the due diligence that you would like to.

Two things can help:

- Judicious use of specialist and experienced IT advisers with a proven track record in negotiating this kind of IT contract (e.g. IT lawyers, specialist accountants and consultants), to help you define what you need, describe it clearly, and compare the offers from IT suppliers.

- A robust and watertight IT outsourcing contract that outlines all of the key issues relating to the relationship, and what redress you would have as a customer if things did not go according to plan. A really good contract will make sure that if this happens, you can exit the relationship quickly, with as little disruption and cost to your organisation as possible.

CHAPTER 3: AGREEING POINTS OF PRINCIPLE

This chapter deals with the essential stage of pinning your IT supplier(s) down to some 'in principle' initial commitments.

This is essential at the early stage of discussions, so that you successfully avoid any unwelcome surprises as the deal progresses. The process takes the form of agreeing key terms.

Your IT supplier(s) will need to agree to these key terms in principle, in writing and before detailed negotiations begin. If you do this, you will have in place a framework from which you can take comfort that contract negotiations are less likely to be a waste of time and money.

Why agreeing key terms matters

As the customer, you can find yourself in a dangerous position if you do not agree some key terms at an early stage.

Some IT suppliers may seek to charge you for 'scoping' your organisation's requirements. (For the record, this, in some cases, could be the IT supplier charging you for pre-sales work they would have to do anyway.) If this happens, you may already feel obliged to agree terms with the IT supplier (even if those terms are not particularly favourable when you look at them more closely). It is important to agree as one of the key terms, that any pre-sales scoping work is either free, or deducted from the eventual price, if you go ahead.

Your IT supplier may have worked for you already, and be 'part of the furniture'. Although you may wish to test the market, this situation can make customers feel dependent on an existing IT supplier. This, in turn, can affect the negotiations about future service contracts. For example, when it then comes to agreeing contractual terms, an incumbent IT supplier may attempt to adopt a relatively uncompromising position on key contractual clauses and terms, in the knowledge that it is probably going to be too disruptive for your organisation to end this relationship and move to another supplier. Agreeing key terms, even with an existing IT supplier, creates a more even playing field, enabling you to compare them with alternatives using rational criteria.

Some customers develop a bias, or emotional attachment, towards a particular IT supplier during contract negotiations, for reasons which may not be objective (for example, if the IT supplier offers to do some initial work for free, although this may be because these costs will simply be recouped later on via higher prices). This may also be because the customer has spent a long time explaining requirements to a particular IT supplier over an extended period, and can't face doing so again to another IT supplier. It may also be that one of the IT suppliers has already started to do some work for the customer (despite no contract having been signed), or it may be that the customer has formed the view that that there are no other IT suppliers that can readily meet specific needs in the time available.

It is perfectly understandable to become emotionally attached to a particular IT supplier early on (i.e. before any contractual documentation has been provided or agreed), such that an organisation simply disregards any other IT suppliers. However, if the organisation has set out key terms from the outset, they will, at least, have some assurance that their decision making is largely objective, and that the organisation will get the best deal that it can.

Not all IT suppliers like key terms

The difficulty with setting out key terms for agreement in principle with one or more IT suppliers, is that it potentially ties IT suppliers down early on, which they may resist. Following are some of the things that IT suppliers can do to keep their options open:

• Ask you to agree to work being done before any contract is signed.

It is true that time is often critical in these types of deals. The IT supplier will often advise you that work needs to be done prior to a contract being signed, citing various reasons. For example, prices can only be held at a certain level for a certain time period and, if detailed contract negotiations take place, then the time period for prices quoted will expire (leading to your organisation paying higher prices!). The IT supplier could suggest that if you wish to avoid paying higher prices, you should agree to work being done now – without a contract – thereby securing lower prices.

The IT supplier could also suggest that it has a certain capacity to do the work now, but if you wait until the contract is signed, there may be a delay in the start date because of commitments to other customers. The IT supplier may argue that engaging in a protracted negotiation process will cause business disruption!

• Ask you to sign the IT supplier's 'standard contract'.

The IT supplier might suggest that, in order to save time and move things forward as quickly as possible, you should simply sign their ' standard terms and conditions' (usually drafted so they are heavily in the supplier's favour), as these have been signed by all of their other customers. The IT supplier may go so far as to say that other major organisations larger than your organisation have signed up to these standard terms and conditions, leaving them puzzled or baffled as to why your organisation will not sign them.

Furthermore, the IT supplier might say that, as you both completely understand the deal and have agreed how the services will be priced, there is no point in engaging lawyers, accountants, procurement personnel or others, since they will only hold up the deal unnecessarily and cost you both more money.

This approach is a danger sign for an organisation and, if this does happen, then you should stand your ground and ask your advisers (e.g. specialist IT outsourcing lawyers, consultants and accountants) to counsel upon the deal. Remember that if the deal is reasonably important and substantial to your organisation, then it is unlikely to be completed from start to finish in a week and there is no harm obtaining advice from your advisers. Whether or not you take this advice is then up to you, but at least you can be aware of what you are getting into and any major pitfalls.

As you can see (and have probably experienced), there are all sorts of 'good reasons' that can be given by an IT supplier as to why your project should start now with either no documentation, or with you signing the 'standard' documentation. Many customers are tempted to go ahead on this basis, but this is likely to be a mistake which will lead to problems later on.

How can you remain in control?

As the customer, you have the money and purchasing power. You can avoid being forced into an unsatisfactory deal by using all or some of the following strategies.

Invite a number of IT suppliers to provide a response to your request for a proposal that outlines your service requirements. Do this, even if you are fairly sure that you wish to stay with your existing supplier and merely negotiate a better deal (i.e. you can shop around).

Issue key terms (these are also referred to as 'points of principle', 'heads of terms' or 'memorandums of understanding'), and be clear that these need to be adhered to if the deal is done. Also be clear that you expect the IT supplier to agree to, and not deviate from, these core terms, and to sign them before full contract negotiations can even begin.

The value of this approach (although it does add another step into the overall process) is that it allows your organisation, at an early stage, to gauge the IT supplier's response. If they query, or reject, these key terms, then you are given an early warning of potential 'deal breakers' or problems and, indeed, an indication of the IT supplier's willingness, or unwillingness, to be flexible or to compromise.

It is better that you find out how your potential IT supplier(s) are going to react to you having clear expectations about quality and process at the beginning of the deal. Otherwise you may find yourself engaging in months of negotiations, and then being left with no option but to accept the IT supplier's best and final offer, since so much time has already been spent on the contract and so much is riding upon it.

Keep at least two IT suppliers at the table, not letting either know the identity of the other(s), or the stage of negotiations, for as long as is reasonably possible, and/or until some kind of contractual documentation is signed with one IT supplier. This keeps your options open for as long as possible. It also deters the IT suppliers from using the fact that they are the only 'game in town' to gain an advantage during contract negotiations, or harden their position as time goes on regarding contractual terms.

Summary

This chapter has reviewed the strategy that some IT suppliers may use to get you to sign a contract (or commission work without a contract). This may be before you have had time to properly assess what they are offering, whether or not you require the relevant IT goods and/or services, and whether or not your organisation can afford this over the long term.

In this chapter, you are advised to get early signup to some key terms in principle. This approach will help you recognise the IT suppliers that are open to working flexibly with you. The investment of time early on in the process could save you significant time and money in the end.

It is, of course, true that a set of 'in principle key terms' are not set in stone. It is often the case that the customer's requirements change during discussions with IT suppliers. However, it remains important that you start off with an objective framework which enables you to make some crucial early comparisons between IT suppliers. It also makes the IT suppliers aware of your 'bottom lines'.

We will look at this issue of bottom lines in the next chapter about deal breakers.

CHAPTER 4: KEY CLAUSES: DEAL BREAKERS, OPTIONS AND WORKAROUNDS

This chapter looks at the sorts of clauses that can often appear in IT contracts, in particular those often referred to as 'show stoppers' or 'deal breakers'.

Deal breakers are clauses which are the most contentious, and which a party will find unacceptable. These clauses may be so unacceptable that a party may refuse to do the deal at all if they are included. However, the other party may deem that these clauses are vital and must be included.

The following are some of the most common deal breakers.

Deal breaker one: Price

You may recall from Chapter 2 how the price of a service contract can escalate if a customer does not clearly specify their requirements, including service levels and quality standards.

You may also recall from Chapter 3 the importance of agreeing early on some in principle key terms. Even though the price may well have been agreed at the point of principle stage, it is often the case that, during negotiations and prior to signature, the customer's requirements have changed as discussions progress.

It frequently happens that after many weeks (if not months) of negotiations about what exactly the customer requires, the customer is nevertheless surprised when it comes to reading/signing the contract; for example:

- How have the deal costs escalated far beyond what was originally anticipated and budgeted for?

- How have the costs of engaging the IT supplier and purchasing its goods and/or services escalated far more than originally anticipated and budgeted for?

Hence, after many months of negotiation, your organisation can be left wondering whether or not the deal makes financial sense any more, and whether or not you are (on reflection) better off staying with your original IT functions and facilities.

If your organisation decides to stay with what it had originally, then it could still be a difficult decision because you will have invested time, effort and resources into negotiations and planning with the IT supplier.

Furthermore, if your organisation has not been very careful to explain the basis upon which negotiations were taking place (e.g. using key terms), the IT supplier may well claim for its wasted costs, time and resources in relation to all work done for your organisation until negotiations broke down (e.g. attending meetings, providing potential IT strategies, ideas and briefing papers, assisting with and crystallising the development of your organisation's ideas, thinking and plans regarding your organisation's IT needs).

Avoiding the price deal breaker

To avoid this deal breaking scenario, the following are essential:

- All costs that your organisation is likely to incur need to be set out clearly at an early stage (especially in the points of principle or key terms).

- Your organisation must be reasonably sure of the goods/services that it requires at the points of principle stage. If you subsequently start to change your mind on an ongoing basis about what your organisation needs and why, you may find that what you actually require becomes unaffordable or unworkable.

- Your organisation must be diligent in terms of scrutinising the IT supplier's costings and asking all relevant questions regarding pricing: the latter may include how prices might increase in the future, or how much more additional goods/services that you might reasonably need could cost in the future.

Deal breaker two: Term and termination

The second type of deal breaker concerns both sides understanding of when and how the contractual relationship between them can be ended.

The IT contract will have been set for a certain time period and can usually only be terminated early for two reasons: material breach of the contract or insolvency of the other party.

Material breach

A material breach is generally a very serious breach of the contract. It is distinct from minor breaches of the contract, such as services being provided a few hours late or services not being exactly as specified. Whether or not there has been a material breach of a contract is often subjective and therefore it is difficult to give an absolute answer about in what circumstances a material breach will definitely have occurred.

Insolvency

If a party cannot pay its debts, or suffers various insolvency related events (e.g. if a liquidator, receiver or administrator is appointed), because of severe financial difficulties, then the other party is often given the option to terminate the agreement.

Terminating the contract: Different perspectives

The IT supplier's position

The IT supplier will often be content with only two termination events (material breach and insolvency) because it will want a long-term contract which is unlikely to be terminated. This will hopefully guarantee revenues for a long period and will look favourable to the IT supplier's bank, investors and shareholders. If the IT supplier is purchased by another IT supplier in the future, it will be able to show that it has a contract with long-term ongoing revenues, which will help to justify the price it wants to sell its business for.

Typically, an IT supplier will propose a five-year deal (or longer), arguing that this is necessary because it will be investing money into the deal in the early years, and will only start to really see a good return on its investment in the later years of the contract. Furthermore, the IT supplier may say that the customer will obtain better, or more favourable, pricing or pricing structures due to the fact that this is a long-term contract (as this will allow the IT supplier to see a return on its investment over a longer rather than a shorter period).

The customer's position

The customer will probably want three key things:

- Additional ways of getting out of the IT outsourcing contract (not just material breach and/or insolvency).

- To be able to get out of the contract much earlier than the five-year term.

- To nevertheless be able to take advantage of the IT supplier's favourable pricing and pricing structures.

For example, your organisation may wish to exit the contract if:

- The services provided and standards are poor, or if there are persistent problems (but these are not so bad that they qualify as a material breach of the contract).

- You want flexibility (for example, you may have merged with, or have been taken over by, a third party, in which case you might want the option to cancel the contract, as the merger or take-over party might have their own IT suppliers). Certainly, no customer will wish to find themselves in a situation where its IT arrangements potentially get in the way of any future merger and acquisition opportunities.

- The IT supplier's prices start to rise, or become uncompetitive, compared to other prices in the market place.

- You no longer need all and/or any part of the IT supplier's goods and/or services (for example, if you decide to move location or to change the way in which your organisation is structured or organised).

- The IT supplier's share ownership changes hands, so that it is controlled by a third party. For example, if an IT supplier is medium-sized, but is then taken over by a global multinational IT supplier which has a different culture and way of doing things. These may include charging more for additional goods or services, and/or adopting a culturally more robust or aggressive approach, or adopting a less personal and individual approach with customers.

- If any actions of the IT supplier materially damage your company's name, goodwill and reputation and/or bring this into disrepute. A general provision such as this may be difficult to negotiate into the IT outsourcing contract, but narrower, specific activities of the IT supplier which damage the reputation of the customer and allow you to terminate, may be possible.

You should consider and/or include provisions in the contract to cater for each of these potential termination events.

Terminating a contract 'at will'

You may also wish to have the right to terminate the contract 'at will' (i.e. for no reason) upon giving the IT supplier a certain period of notice (for example, six months).

The IT supplier is likely to resist such an option, since this would make the contract effectively a six-month rolling contract (rather than a five-year deal).

One solution that is often utilised is that the customer is able to terminate 'at will', but only on the payment of a termination fee to the IT supplier. This termination fee is usually set at a certain amount which the parties agree in advance. The termination fee could be, for example:

- The customer agreeing to pay the IT supplier a fixed fee which is based upon a certain proportion of the remaining term of the contract (but not the whole of the remaining term of the contract).

The IT supplier should be compensated for the contract being terminated 'at will', but should not be entitled to all of the money for the remaining term of the contract, since the IT supplier would not be actually incurring costs and expenses in doing the work for this remaining period of the contract. The IT supplier may also be able to redeploy its staff to work for one of its other customers for the remaining terms of the contract.

The termination fee could also be:

• The lost profit that the IT supplier has incurred, minus a discount for accelerated payment. The lost profit is likely to be much less than the amount which was due from the customer for the remaining term, since only a proportion of this would constitute profit for the IT supplier.

Of course, most customers would like to be able to terminate 'at will' without any cost, but this is unlikely to be acceptable to the IT supplier. Negotiating a termination fee into the IT outsourcing contract at least gives your organisation the option to exit the IT outsourcing contract.

Renewal

Your organisation may wish to negotiate into the IT outsourcing contract the right to renewal, on certain agreed terms, after the initial contract period (perhaps similar to the ones already in existence in the original contract). This will be dependent on you providing a notice of renewal within a reasonable period of the end of the original contract. However, there may be some contentious terms e.g. price, in that the IT supplier may not be willing to hold prices at the same level as they were at the start of the original contract, and may want to charge significantly more (since they will be aware that the cost of your organisation engaging a completely new IT supplier may be far more expensive than paying slightly more to the existing IT supplier). Hence, renewal terms should be agreed as much as possible in advance and included in the original IT outsourcing contract.

Deal breaker three: Exclusions and limitations of liability

These are deal breaker clauses that aim to make the IT supplier responsible for the financial consequences of disruption to your organisation – which could happen as a result of the IT supplier's service or lack of it.

If an IT supplier provides software, and that software goes wrong, then the impact could be catastrophic for your organisation.

You could, in principle, claim for the losses you have incurred. In theory, this claim could amount to the whole value of your organisation, if the problem with the software was proven to have led to the collapse of your organisation.

For example, if software provided by an IT supplier to a bank went wrong, such that the bank's customers could not obtain money from cash machines, then the losses to the bank relating to customers going to other banks; loss of reputation; and potential collapse of the bank, could be traced back to the software and the IT supplier.

The IT supplier, having only charged the customer a certain amount for the software, could then find that it was potentially responsible for billions of pounds worth of losses if the software went wrong (and the bank collapsed).

Capping liability

For obvious reasons, an IT supplier will often want to cap its total liability under the contract. The most usual caps include:

*   The annual contract price

*   The total contract price

*   Another pre-agreed fixed sum.

The cap represents the maximum amount that the IT supplier would have to pay if you sued them for being in breach of the contract. This could be, for example, if the software they supplied went wrong and had significant consequences for your organisation.

If the IT supplier is paid a certain amount, then it could be agreed that this amount is also the cap. For example, if you pay the IT supplier one million pounds in a year, then you could agree that the IT supplier's cap is one million pounds, such that if your organisation sues for breach of the IT outsourcing contract, then they will not be responsible for any losses suffered by the customer which exceed that amount (i.e. which exceed one million pounds). Therefore, if the software does go wrong (and in this example causes £10 million worth of damage), then the IT supplier's liability is capped (in this example, at one million pounds) and losses over and above that amount (in this example, £9 million) will be your responsibility (even though all of this loss was caused by the IT supplier).

The reason why this cap is included, is because it does not make business sense for an IT supplier to enter into a contract for one million pounds per year and yet be responsible on an unlimited basis for liability, which could be tens or hundreds of millions of pounds. The amount received under the IT contract by the IT supplier would be disproportionate to the amount of risk it would be assuming by entering into such a contract.

It is unlikely that an IT supplier will enter into an IT transaction where its liability is not capped or limited in some way. Negotiations about the level of the cap often start at around the contract price, and tend to go up in multiples of the contract price (e.g. 150% of contract price).

Customers will need to accept that there will always be a balance between how much the IT supplier is paid and how much they are prepared to be responsible for. So why is this a deal breaker?

The deal breaker is often the level of the cap. As the customer, you may want the cap to be very high, but the supplier will usually only accept a cap at a much lower level.

The IT supplier may also argue that if you want to have a higher cap on liability, then the price of the overall contract will need to go up (in order to enable the supplier to take on more risk and also perhaps obtain more insurance to cover its increased level of responsibility over and above the insurance that the supplier ordinarily has in place for its business). Note that if the insurance provided by the IT supplier is in excess of its liability cap, then this does not automatically prevent the IT supplier's cap from being fair and reasonable.[3]

Your organisation need to be clear about exactly what the cap is at a very early stage, rather than being surprised to see a very low cap in contractual documentation which appears after many months of negotiations (since this may then become a deal breaker if the IT supplier refuses to increase such a cap, or asks for prices to be increased in the event of you wanting an increased cap).

What the cap can/cannot cover

IT outsourcing contracts will generally contain the following sorts of provisions:

- Neither party may limit, or exclude, its liability for death or personal injury caused by its negligence. This cannot be excluded under English law.

- The IT supplier (and in some cases the customer) may exclude their liability for consequential, indirect and special losses. These are losses which are, in general, 'knock-on' losses from the breach in question. For example, if a piece of software fails for an hour, and the customer is a bank, then the consequential losses could include:

   ○ The bank's staff being unable to process transactions for an hour (therefore the bank paying wages for staff that were unable to work).

   ○ The bank losing customers who decide to go to another bank because they could not get what they wanted during that hour.

---

[3] Shepherd Homes Ltd v Encia (2007) states that insurance provisions in a contract can affect the validity of a liability cap.

○ The time that the bank spent dealing with complaints.

○ The loss of reputation, or goodwill, of the bank with its customers (together with any negative press comment).

The point to remember here is that there can be a whole chain of knock-on losses; and there must come a point where the IT supplier says that the losses are not reasonably foreseeable, or are too remote from the default in question to be claimable by the customer. The point of the clause about excluding consequential losses is to draw that line in as much detail as possible.

Your organisation might want to also add its own caps and exclusions into the IT outsourcing contract so that it can benefit from these.

Case law about capping liability

Some situations cannot be foreseen, so the question of exactly where the line about the extent of consequential losses is actually drawn will depend on the IT supplier default in question and the circumstances surrounding it. That means there may still be some negotiation about redress, even though the contract contains a limitation of liability clause.

For example, there are plenty of cases where a customer has agreed to an IT supplier cap on liability and then, once a major default has occurred which is the IT supplier's fault and where enormous losses have been sustained by the customer, they have sought to challenge the cap in court as being unreasonable. For example, if an IT supplier's cap is £100,000 and the customer suffers £50 million in losses due to the IT supplier's default, then often the customer will seek to challenge the validity of the cap.[4]

---

[4] Leading cases relating to customers challenging liability caps include: St Albans City and District Council v ICL (1996); Anglo Group Plc v Winther Browne & Co Limited (2000); Watford Electronics v Sanderson (2001); Alfred McAlpine v Tilebox (2005) and Internet Broadcasting Corporation v Mar LLC (2009).

Case law suggests that whether or not the cap will be upheld by the courts depends upon the circumstances in each case.

IT suppliers must therefore be careful when setting caps. They cannot be so low as to be adjudged to be unreasonable if the contract were to ever be scrutinised by the courts.

The customer should be fully aware of what exactly the cap means and its effect. If you go to court to try to overturn and invalidate a cap, when a major IT loss has occurred, you are unlikely to be regarded favourably by the court if you show no understanding of the potential impact of the liability exclusion on how you do business.[5]

Finally, when drafting exclusion and limitation clauses, it is important to ensure that they are drafted in plain English and explicitly state what liability is intended to be excluded or limited.

An evaluation should be carried out as to what potential losses could be classified as direct; and what losses could be classified as indirect or consequential; and then the clauses should be carefully drafted accordingly.

If 'loss of profits' is to be excluded, then (based upon case law) this should be done separately from an exclusion of indirect or consequential losses. Wording which links loss of profits with indirect, or consequential, losses should be avoided. Hence, wording such as 'no liability for indirect or consequential losses such as loss of profits' or an exclusion for 'loss of profits, or other indirect, or consequential, losses' should be avoided.

If the limitation or exclusion is to be included in standard terms of business and is not negotiated then it must also satisfy the reasonability requirements of the Unfair Contract Terms Act 1977.

Your organisation should also agree elements of the IT outsourcing contract which are not subject to the cap (for

---

[5] Anglo Group Plc v Winther Browne & Co Limited (2000); Watford Electronics v Sanderson (2001).

example, if the IT supplier breaches confidentiality or intellectual property clauses in the contract).

Deal breaker four: Intellectual property

It is important for the parties to talk about and agree intellectual property clauses (e.g. regarding patents, copyright, trademarks, etc.), and ownership of intellectual property.

Your organisation will want to own the intellectual property that is created for it by the IT supplier during the course of the IT contract. This will mean that the IT supplier cannot use this intellectual property for itself or for any of its other customers (including your competitors). This also allows you to use the intellectual property created for you (e.g. with other IT suppliers).

The IT supplier will normally resist such a clause to the extent that it will not want you to have ownership of all intellectual property used or produced by it during the course of the contract. For example, the IT supplier may use intellectual property which was in existence before the contract with your organisation and belongs to third parties or is licensed to the IT supplier to use generally. It may also use intellectual property which it has created outside the scope of your contract, but which it uses as part of providing IT goods and services to you under your contract (supplier intellectual property).

Even if you agree that your organisation cannot own the supplier intellectual property, provisions need to be added to the IT outsourcing contract to ensure that your organisation is authorised to use it throughout the term of the contract. This also needs to apply after the contract, to the extent that this is necessary in order for you to be able to use the intellectual property which your organisation owns pursuant to the contract. For example, in order to use intellectual property owned by you and created for you by the IT supplier during the contract, you may need to make use of supplier intellectual property.

Talks about intellectual property can become complex and protracted particularly if, for example, the IT supplier wants the intellectual property that it has developed for you (and for which you have paid), for its other customers, including your competitors (thereby saving the IT supplier development and production costs), and this may be something which you object to.[6]

Summary

This section has looked at four key types of deal breaker in an IT outsourcing contract: price; term and termination; exclusions and limitations of liability; and intellectual property. The key message is that it is important that you, as the customer, understand these clauses, why they appear, and their potential impact on your organisation.

---

[6] See problems that can arise with intellectual property in Clearsprings Management Limited v Business Linx Ltd (2005) EWHC 1487 (Ch).

CHAPTER 5: AGREEING THE IT OUTSOURCING CONTRACT

This chapter looks at preparing, negotiating and agreeing the IT outsourcing contract.

As the preceding chapters suggest, before you even look at an IT outsourcing contract, it is likely that you will have already done a lot of preparatory work. This will have included scouring the market for suitable IT suppliers, inviting them to submit proposals, meeting and interviewing them, doing further checks on them (such as visiting reference sites and speaking with some of their customers), and agreeing key terms in principle with the two or more IT suppliers that you choose to negotiate with. It is also important to ensure that any so called 'deal breakers' have been addressed and agreed to your satisfaction.

Putting an IT outsourcing contract in place

It is worth noting that if the terms of an IT outsourcing contract are disputed by you and/or the IT supplier, then the costs of litigation can be very high which can eat into any savings that you have made by entering into the IT outsourcing contract in the first place. Hence, it is essential that the IT outsourcing contract is properly drafted and covers all of the relevant issues, so as to minimise the risks of any disputes arising.

The following are some key issues to consider.

Timetable

It is advisable to lay out a set timetable for each stage of the process.

The IT outsourcing contract, depending on its value, might take anywhere from a few weeks to many months to prepare, negotiate, amend and finalise before both parties are satisfied with it. If any third party approvals or permissions are required (such as any governmental or regulatory approval), or if the IT outsourcing contract is to span different countries, then this can add further time to the process.

It is important to leave grace periods (slippage time) at the end of each stage. This is to cater for any unexpected issues which may arise and also major holidays (such as Christmas, Easter and the summer holiday period), personal holidays or working practices in different countries which all mean that key people and advisers are unavailable and getting decisions made takes longer than normal.

Roles

In any major outsourcing deal, a number of different people may be involved, including:

- Industry and IT consultants who can help you come to a decision about which IT suppliers to consider and why.

- Your own senior personnel (such as board directors) who are authorised to discuss your business requirements with IT suppliers in broad terms; and lead the IT outsourcing process for your organisation.

- Your finance director or senior accountant should also be involved in assessing the financial nature of the IT outsourcing contract. This role may extend beyond price structuring to include an analysis of issues, such as VAT and depreciation, and an examination of the contract to ensure that the cost savings which you hope to achieve can be achieved by the IT outsourcing contract as drafted.

- Procurement and compliance professionals with experience of tendering processes, knowledge of the IT supply market, and the competence to ensure that your IT procurement process is fair (i.e. complies with all relevant regulations and laws). These professionals will be invaluable in the initial stages of the process and may also be involved in negotiating and/or implementing the IT outsourcing contract itself.

- Your commercial managers who you task with overseeing the day-to-day progress of the project from the start, up to and including the signing of the IT outsourcing contract. As these managers are usually the people who manage the IT outsourcing contract after it is signed, it is helpful if they have sufficient input into the terms of the IT outsourcing contract and understand how it has been constructed.

- Specialist IT outsourcing lawyers who are engaged in preparing the IT outsourcing contract and provide legal expertise and industry knowledge about how such specialist contracts are structured. This will ensure that the contract is legally valid and enforceable and covers all the key issues.

- Your IT director/chief information officer who may have the role of overseeing the project, making IT strategic decisions, liaising with the technical staff at the IT supplier, and becoming involved in negotiations. These staff may hold the brief for reporting to the board on progress and major governance issues which arise.

The importance of good communications

As so many people are likely to be involved in a medium to high value outsourcing deal, it is imperative that everyone is kept updated and informed about what is happening, and that they have some input into the decision-making processes. Major issues and arguments tend to arise when:

- Individuals at your organisation have unilaterally agreed points with the IT supplier, without discussing and agreeing these with your own team.

- Too many personnel at your organisation talk to the IT supplier, which leads to misunderstandings and crossed wires. Ideally, comments from everyone at your organisation should be gathered, discussed internally by personnel, filtered, and then channelled through a spokesperson (e.g. your nominated project leader, managing director, chief executive officer, finance director or specialist IT outsourcing lawyer). This works more effectively than lots of disparate comments being made to the IT supplier.

- Your bargaining positions have been inadvertently disclosed to the IT supplier (such as which other IT suppliers are being considered and also the prices offered by others).

Cost

The costs of agreeing an IT outsourcing deal will depend to a large extent on the value of the deal.

If the IT outsourcing deal is of extremely high value (e.g. £100 million plus), then it is likely to require a significant amount of preparation (including 'due diligence' about the potential IT suppliers, their status, capability and ability to successfully perform the contract), involve significant numbers of personnel, and might involve a number of countries.

For IT outsourcing deals of around £20 million, the legal fees tend to come in at between 0.25%–1% depending on the complexity of the deal and the time it takes to reach agreement.

For example, in a recent £70 million deal spanning a number of EU countries, the legal fees for preparing and negotiating the IT outsourcing contract were in the region of £250,000, excluding VAT.

Typically, the legal costs for a smaller IT outsourcing deal in the UK alone are unlikely to be much less than £10,000, plus VAT.

In addition to legal fees, major IT outsourcing contract negotiations will need to factor in the costs of personnel, such as IT consultants, accountants, other advisers and also your own staff time at your organisation.

You can see from the above, that if you are considering an IT outsourcing project, then you will need to budget for the deal costs, and factor them into your project business case to ensure that the deal will still deliver the cost savings you may be seeking.

Other legal issues

Detailed below are some of the key legal issues that arise in IT outsourcing contract negotiations.

Escrow arrangements

Putting materials or documents in 'escrow' means leaving them with a third party (often called an escrow agent). This is important in the following sort of situation.

If an IT supplier is providing software for your organisation, the source code to that software (i.e. the computer language program) will not be made available to you. This is firstly because the computer program is the IT supplier's intellectual property; and secondly because if the program were to be disclosed to any unauthorised parties, then it would be easy to copy and distribute, which could seriously damage the IT supplier's business.

However, you as the customer may need access to this source code to maintain your software if your IT supplier breaches the IT contract and fails to maintain the software for you.

The usual compromise is that both parties enter into a source code escrow agreement whereby the source code is kept by an independent third party. If the IT supplier becomes insolvent, or fails to maintain the software due to a breach of the IT contract, then the escrow agent will release the source code to you (solely for the purpose of maintaining your software).

Employment law

If you are outsourcing your IT department, such that your current employees will no longer be needed, then it is imperative that you consider employment legislation, particularly the Transfer of Undertakings (Protection of Employment) Regulations 2006 (TUPE) and similar employment related legislation.

In this example, under TUPE, if the employees in your IT department transfer to the IT supplier, then they will become employees of the IT supplier. This can have a number of consequences, including the IT supplier being responsible for all of your organisation's past defaults (if any) regarding such employees (including any claims by such employees against your organisation).

As a consequence of the above, detailed provisions and indemnities will need to be added to the contract, such that the IT supplier is, in effect, reimbursed from any employment-related claims by such employees, prior to the date of their transfer to the IT supplier, together with any monies which the IT supplier pays out to those employees regarding certain issues (e.g. any redundancy costs).

At the end of the contract, it may be that your organisation is obliged under TUPE to take on the IT supplier's employees that spend all or most of their time working for you. In this case, terms will need to be added to the contract, so that your organisation is properly reimbursed for taking on such employees (in a similar way to the way in which the IT supplier is reimbursed for taking on your organisation's employees at the start of the IT outsourcing contract). Note also that pensions of transferring employees, and what happens to these pensions, will also need to be dealt with.

Data protection and data issues

The Data Protection Act 1998 contains provisions relating to the protection of personal data. Key considerations for your organisation include:

- Are you gathering and processing personal data (i.e. names and addresses of individuals)? Have you obtained the consent of those individuals to process that personal data (or can you rely on other conditions in the Data Protection Act which allow you to process such data)? Are you transferring this data outside the European Union? If so, your organisation will need to take extra precautions, including entering into contracts containing certain clauses with the offshore parties that you are doing business with. This is important because in respect of personal data, you will generally be primarily responsible under the Data

Protection Act 1998 for the defaults of your offshore supplier in processing that personal data for you.

• Are you gathering and processing sensitive personal data (which includes, amongst other things, an individual's health records or criminal records or religious beliefs)? If so, additional precautions will need to be taken, including obtaining the individual's express consent to process such sensitive data.

• Ensuring that all of your data and information (including subsequent updates and modifications) is owned by you at all times and that you have access to and use of it. This data should also be returned to you at the end of the IT outsourcing contract.[7]

Step in rights

If the IT supplier is in material default (or is likely to be so), then you might want the right for you or a replacement supplier to 'step in' to perform the IT supplier's obligations. However, this can be difficult to achieve in practice because the very reason you outsourced your IT in the first place, was as you wanted that IT supplier to deal with this (and any problems relating to it). Hence, before asking for 'step in' rights, be sure about whether you can actually use or implement this option in practice.

Offshoring abroad

The themes in this book also apply to IT outsourcing abroad (offshoring). Additional issues and challenges arise regarding offshoring, which include the following:

• **The enforceability of contracts.** Taking action against a party based in India, for example, may be more difficult than doing so in the UK.

---

[7] Disputes can occur as to who owns the data, if this is not specifically provided for in the contract. See Cureton v Mark Insulations (2006) EWCH 2279 (QB).

- **Monitoring.** Keeping track of the work that is being done, and monitoring the quality of the service, can be more challenging if you do not have the time, resources or additional money to regularly visit and monitor your IT supplier at their offshore location.

- **Cultural issues.** You may be used to working, or having your IT services delivered, in a particular way. This may change according to the offshore IT supplier's internal working culture, and the way that business is typically done where they are based (which may be very different to how it is done in the UK).

- **Data protection and regulatory issues** will also need to be addressed.

- **Communication and language.** Key problems that arise include misunderstandings about the importance of deadlines; how long it takes to get problems resolved; and the delivery of more subjective service standards. Offshore IT suppliers may say that your requirements were not fully explained, and that they were working on inaccurate, incomplete or out-of-date information.

IT offshoring can bring many benefits to customers, but challenges must be identified early on, and addressed quickly and firmly, if an IT offshoring relationship is to work well. Finally, it is important to appreciate that these kinds of problems are very likely to occur, regardless of where the fault lies.

Specialist IT outsourcing lawyers

Specialist IT outsourcing lawyers have a good knowledge of specialist IT law and the IT industry, and may be able to get the best deal for you.

However, many organisations will automatically engage their local or normal firm of solicitors (even if that firm has little, or no, real specialist experience in this area). This can be a mistake.

Therefore:

1   Select a law firm or lawyer that specialises in this area.

2   Do **not** make your final decision on a lawyer on price or hourly rates alone. The specialist IT outsourcing lawyers that are likely to get you the best long-term deal, will not necessarily be the cheapest!

Selecting your lawyers is critical because the IT supplier is likely to have its own IT specialist lawyers to argue its case.

Summary

This chapter has outlined some of the issues which many customers may not immediately consider when pursuing an outsourcing project. It is useful to enter into negotiations being reasonably confident about the sorts of issues that are likely to arise, and what your organisation's response to them is likely to be. Experienced and specialist advisers are invaluable, especially in medium to large IT outsourcing deals.

CHAPTER 6: MANAGING THE RELATIONSHIP: TYPICAL PROBLEMS AND SOLUTIONS

This chapter outlines some of the key 'bear traps' to look out for once you have entered into an IT outsourcing contract, and describes how to try and pre-empt conflicts with your IT supplier.

Making changes to your IT outsourcing contract

Changes will normally be required in the outsourcing arrangement for various reasons, including the following:

- Your organisation's business needs might have changed.

- Your organisation may want its IT support provided in a different (perhaps more cost-effective) way.

- You may no longer need certain services.

In most IT outsourcing contracts, there is a change request procedure. Most contracts will require changes to be documented for cost, legal and audit purposes.

Problems can occur when making changes to your service and these can have a contractual implication. The most common problems include:

- **Cost increases.** Costs can escalate as more and more changes are requested, particularly if the original specification was not exactly what you wanted, or if the original specification was incomplete. These cost increases can eat into the financial savings that you may have counted on, unless they can be offset in other ways.

- **Delays.** Changes can mean delays to the implementation of the new IT service, which can put the whole implementation process back (and out of line with performance standards), as well as potentially having a knock-on effect to other parts of your business.

- **Disputes.** Disputes and litigation can arise as a result of costs increasing and delays occurring, especially where (as is often the case) each party believes that the cost increases/delays are the other party's fault.

If changes to your IT outsourcing arrangement affect the price of the service and/or the standards of the project; and eventually lead to a dispute, what can you do?

One option is court action, but the IT outsourcing contract normally provides other dispute resolution mechanisms. For example, escalation, where if the dispute cannot be resolved at a lower level within certain timescales, it is escalated all the way up to the chief executive officers.

Failing resolution, the parties could provide for (i) mediation – where the parties can discuss and deal with their issues in a confidential environment with a mediator, to try to facilitate a negotiated solution; and/or (ii) arbitration – where the parties can submit to an arbitration process, whereby the decision of the arbitrator is final and binding (unless an obvious error has been made).

If immediate court action is required (for example, if confidential information is disclosed, or your IP is infringed by your IT supplier), then your organisation may opt to take out an injunction. However, legal fees for injunctions can be high and there is no guarantee of success.[8] Note that other dispute mechanisms do exist, such as expert determination.

In order to avoid disputes, the next section looks at service standards and service level agreements within IT outsourcing contracts.

Service standards and service level agreements

Service level agreements lay out the service standards, key performance indicators and benchmarks for your outsourced IT service. They also include the requirement for your IT supplier

---

[8] See Vertex Data Science Limited v Powergen Retail Limited (2006) EWHC 1340 (Comm) where an injunction was not granted in an outsourcing dispute.

to provide regular data about performance, so that you can monitor service standards.

If your IT outsourcing contract does not have a service level agreement, then it will be more difficult for you to establish and prove objectively that service standards are declining, inadequate or unsatisfactory.

The service level agreement will usually be included in a schedule to the outsourcing agreement and will set out the following:

- **Standards to be achieved.** For example, the service level agreement might state that the IT availability must be 99% or more over any set period.

- **Breached standards.** The service level agreement will document what will happen if service standards are not met. A common approach to this issue is for the IT supplier to issue the customer with service credits, which are:

  ○ Fixed amounts of money.

  ○ Pre-agreed as part of the IT outsourcing negotiations.

  ○ Aimed at compensating your organisation for any losses suffered because service standards do not meet pre-agreed levels.

  ○ Aimed at helping both parties avoid disputes, as the action to be taken in respect of under-performance is pre-agreed.

  ○ Linked directly to performance standards and their timescale.

For example, if a service standard (e.g. availability of IT) is below the pre-agreed level of 99%, then it may be agreed that £x is paid for every percentage point (or part thereof) that the service falls below 99%.

Likewise, if the service standard is to be met over a given period of time (e.g. a month or a quarter), then the service credit (if applicable) is paid over the same period.

Service credits are discussed in greater detail below, together with their relationship to service standards and monitoring.

Key issues to consider when developing your service level agreement

In the most effective service level agreements, there are typically between four and 10 service levels, or key performance indicators.

Too many service levels, or key performance indicators, (e.g. 20 plus) can create the following problems: measurement can be cumbersome and difficult to keep track of, data becomes difficult to understand and interpret without dedicated analytical support; significant extra work and resources will then need to be dedicated by the IT supplier to this task. This will either cost you more, or it will mean that the IT supplier must focus its resources on counting activities, rather than more directly on providing better services.

Service standards should be measured over a reasonable period of time (typically a month or a quarter) in order to measure trends (rather than blips). The IT supplier will typically only pay service credits for service standards which are not met over an agreed set period of a month, or a quarter (rather than being penalised for blips over a day or a week).

You may want the option to change service standards over the term of the contract, particularly if you wish to replace those standards which are met regularly (and which the IT supplier has got used to meeting) with others that are not met regularly. This approach will help you to ensure that your IT supplier is committed to constantly improving the service offered.

On the matter of service credits (which are pre-agreed sums of money for breaches of pre-agreed service levels), the service level agreement or outsourcing contract should make it clear that:

•   There should be no double counting of service credits (i.e. several separate service credits should not be payable for essentially the same service level standard breach). Service credits are aimed at helping both parties to manage the relationship on a day-to-day basis. However, they should not cap or limit your right to claim damages or losses regarding a major breach of the outsourcing contract, or the service level agreement (i.e. they should not form your exclusive remedy in respect of service breaches). As a customer, you will not want to be limited to claiming relatively small service credits, if and when major breaches of the IT outsourcing contract, or service level agreement, occur.

• The service credits that your organisation can claim in any set period are capped (typically at around 5%–15% of the amount payable by your organisation to the supplier over that set period). This means that:

  ○ The IT supplier does not completely lose all of its profit for any set period, simply due to some service level breaches. This is important because, if your organisation has an IT supplier that is essentially not making any money out of your contract, then it is likely to be demotivated and may well focus its resources and best staff upon other more lucrative contracts with other customers.

• You are not tempted to try to recover all, or a substantial amount, of monies payable to the IT supplier, by making service level standard complaints (for example, if you use the claiming of service credits as a way of obtaining an unofficial discount on services provided).

Your organisation should also consider IT supplier incentivisation clauses which incentivise the IT supplier to provide benefits to your organisation. For example, if the IT supplier can identify cost savings or efficiencies, then you might share those cost savings. If these are particularly beneficial, you may reward the IT supplier by continuing to spend your organisation's share of the cost savings with them. If you don't consider this, then the IT supplier has no incentive at all to point out cost savings to you, since it will simply lose money by doing so.

Specific bonus payments which are received directly by certain staff at the IT supplier, for particularly good performance on your organisation's IT outsourcing contract, are another incentivisation clause.

Summary

This chapter has focused on the key processes available to manage your relationship with your IT supplier, in particular: service level agreements (including key performance indicators), and the use of service credits.

Ultimately, it is down to your organisation as the customer, to decide where and how you want your IT supplier to focus time and resources. You may wish to consider the benefits you are seeking by setting key performance indicators.

Finally, there may be 'softer' ways of ensuring that high quality and responsiveness is maintained; for example, by focusing on the quality of the relationship or regularity of meetings between you and your IT supplier, and considering incentivisation schemes which increase goodwill and mutual trust, and benefit both your organisation and the IT supplier.

CHAPTER 7: ENDING THE IT OUTSOURCING RELATIONSHIP

Termination

All IT outsourcing arrangements will sooner or later come to an end. This chapter outlines how to manage the end of your IT outsourcing relationship, with as little disruption to your business as possible.

Chapter 4 described the two fundamental reasons for terminating an IT outsourcing contract (material breach of contract and insolvency of either party); and also outlined possible additional clauses that you, as the customer, may wish to negotiate into your agreement.

However, terminating your IT outsourcing contract could leave you facing some difficulties. For example, if you terminate the contract for material breach, and there is subsequently found to be a breach – but not one so serious as to qualify as a material breach, then the IT supplier may allege that you have terminated without justification. This means that your organisation itself is then in material breach of the contract. The IT supplier may then claim all the losses, costs and expenses that it might have suffered as a result of such unjustified termination[9].

There is usually a strong interdependency between your organisation and your IT supplier, especially where the contract has run for some time. Ending this relationship abruptly, can cause enormous disruption to both parties.

Ending an IT outsourcing relationship may mean that you need to engage a replacement IT supplier. This new IT supplier may see that your organisation is 'in distress', and use this to gain advantage. For example, they may seek to charge a premium for services; or disclaim liability for some services/quality

---

[9] This happened in the case of Peregrine Systems v Steria (2004) EWHC 275 (TCC).

standards provided, saying that their capacity to provide may be limited by the previous IT supplier's legacy goods, for which the replacement supplier does not want to be responsible.

Nevertheless, if you are considering terminating an IT outsourcing contract and you do not have the in-house resources, you need to have the necessary plans in place to be able to receive IT goods and services (including the appointment of a replacement IT supplier on agreed contractual terms) in the future.

A good ending

Ending IT outsourcing contracts can always cause some business disruption. To minimise disruption, the IT outsourcing contract should include a well thought out exit plan.

The exit plan should be agreed in writing <u>at the start</u> of the IT contract, and form part of the contract. Your organisation's bargaining position, and relationship with the IT supplier, are likely to be better at the start of the contract than at the end of the contract, when you are separating.

The exit plan should:

- Explain the obligations of the parties, if and when, termination or expiry occurs.

- Cover issues, such as the IT supplier doing all the work that you reasonably request to transfer the IT services back to your organisation, or to a replacement IT supplier nominated by you, within relevant timescales. This will require the IT supplier to:

  ○ Provide details of any existing projects, their current status and any further work that needs to be done on them.

  ○ Not start any new projects or incur any unnecessary costs or expenses on existing projects.

  ○ Co-operate with your organisation and provide relevant information and reasonable assistance to you and/or any replacement IT supplier (including in respect of public relations).

- Be updated at regular intervals throughout the project by the IT supplier (outlining changes and new positions or systems), so that if termination occurs abruptly then you and your IT supplier have a relatively up-to-date exit plan to follow.

- Be 'fault neutral'. This means that the exit plan should include the provision that the IT supplier should be paid for this work – regardless of why the contract was terminated and/or whose fault this might have been. This is because implementation of the exit plan and any contractual breach should be treated as completely separate issues.

  This is for several reasons, including:

  ○ Even if the contract had gone to plan, the IT supplier would have been paid for work on the exit plan at expiry of the contract.

  ○ The importance of ensuring business as usual.

  ○ The fact that any action by you against the IT supplier for losses incurred, is likely to take longer than exiting the arrangement.

If you stay in an unworkable relationship with your IT supplier, until you have been paid for the impact of poor performance, this may have a detrimental effect on your business. It is often better to exit and find a new supplier; and pursue any action for damages as a separate process. However, if a replacement IT supplier is to take over, then it should be fully contracted to you to provide replacement IT services, before you terminate your old IT outsourcing contract.

Finally, the fees and/or charging agreement relating to your IT supplier's implementation of the agreed exit plan, should also be agreed at the start of the IT outsourcing contract, as part of the key terms. This avoids you being charged additional, or higher, fees, if this is the last piece of business that you provide to your IT supplier.

Summary

The keys to a satisfactory contract end are both hard and soft. The soft side includes: ongoing communications and trying not to let things become personal. The hard side includes: having a clear exit plan in your IT outsourcing contract; giving fair notice; separating the process of exiting the contract from wider issues about possible compensation; contracting with a replacement IT supplier before ending your existing contract; and managing public relations. Finally, but of utmost importance, it is vital to seek advice before terminating your IT outsourcing contract, to ensure that you are fully aware of the legal and other consequences of doing so.

CHAPTER 8: CONCLUSIONS AND KEY LEARNING POINTS

This short, legal and practical guide to IT outsourcing seeks to offer you some key tips on entering into (and exiting) an IT outsourcing contract, in a way that will save both parties disruption and money.

Outlined below are the key questions raised in each of the chapters.

Chapter 1	Why is your organisation outsourcing? What benefits will outsourcing bring? What kinds of cost savings are likely to be realised? Does IT outsourcing make financial sense for your organisation?
Chapter 2	How do you go about choosing your IT outsourcing supplier? What can go wrong when choosing your IT outsourcing supplier?
Chapter 3	The benefits of agreeing key terms up front. What can go wrong if you do not agree key terms up front?
Chapter 4	Deal breaker clauses: What are they and how can you deal with them?
Chapter 5	How do you go about putting an IT outsourcing contract in place – who does what? What other legal issues should your organisation consider regarding IT outsourcing, in addition to issues such as price and standard of services?

Chapter 6	How can your organisation manage the IT outsourcing relationship? The benefits of using service level agreements.
Chapter 7	Ending the IT outsourcing relationship – how can your organisation do this with minimal business disruption?

The IT outsourcing contract (including the service level agreement), provides the important bridge between you, the customer, and your IT supplier.

It is vital that your IT outsourcing contract is drafted properly, so that it caters for all of your generic and individual requirements. Organisations quickly become highly dependent upon their IT supplier, and the IT outsourcing contract is the framework within which you can negotiate changes in a way that will ensure minimal disruption, additional costs and/or delays.

Terminating an IT outsourcing contract is often difficult, but the process can be made manageable, so long as the contract contains a comprehensive exit plan, to ensure a smooth transition of services back to your organisation or to a replacement IT supplier.

Finally, you will know only too well that good IT is the backbone of a successful organisation. If you decide that managing your own IT function is not your core business (as many medium- to large-sized organisations do), and that the way forward is to outsource the function, then it is important to identify early on what sort of specialist expert legal and other advice you might wish to access and obtain. This will ensure that the process goes smoothly and that you do not store up unexpected problems (or costs) for the future.

ITG RESOURCES

IT Governance Ltd sources, creates and delivers products and services to meet the real-world, evolving IT governance needs of today's organisations, directors, managers and practitioners. The ITG website (*www.itgovernance.co.uk*) is the international one-stop-shop for corporate and IT governance information, advice, guidance, books, tools, training and consultancy.

www.itgovernance.co.uk/it-outsourcing.aspx is the information page on our website for our outsourcing resources.

Other Websites

Books and tools published by IT Governance Publishing (ITGP) are available from all business booksellers and are also immediately available from the following websites:

www.itgovernance.co.uk/catalog/355 provides information and online purchasing facilities for every currently available book published by ITGP.

www.itgovernanceusa.com is a US$-based website that delivers the full range of IT Governance products to North America, and ships from within the continental US.

www.itgovernanceasia.com provides a selected range of ITGP products specifically for customers in South Asia.

www.27001.com is the IT Governance Ltd website that deals specifically with information security management, and ships from within the continental US.

Pocket Guides

For full details of the entire range of pocket guides, simply follow the links at *www.itgovernance.co.uk/publishing.aspx.*

Toolkits

ITG's unique range of toolkits includes the IT *Governance Framework Toolkit*, which contains all the tools and guidance that you will need in order to develop and implement an appropriate IT governance framework for your organisation. Full details can be found at *www.itgovernance.co.uk/products/519.*

For a free paper on how to use the proprietary Calder-Moir IT Governance Framework, and for a free trial version of the toolkit, see *www.itgovernance.co.uk/calder_moir.aspx.*

There is also a wide range of toolkits to simplify implementation of management systems, such as an ISO/IEC 27001 ISMS or a BS25999 BCMS, and these can all be viewed and purchased online at: *www.itgovernance.co.uk/catalog/1.*

Best Practice Reports

ITG's range of Best Practice Reports is now at *www.itgovernance.co.uk/best-practice-reports.aspx.* These offer you essential, pertinent, expertly researched information on an increasing number of key issues including Web 2.0 and Green IT.

Training and Consultancy

IT Governance also offers training and consultancy services across the entire spectrum of disciplines in the information governance arena. Details of training courses can be accessed at *www.itgovernance.co.uk/training.aspx* and descriptions of our consultancy services can be found at *www.itgovernance.co.uk/consulting.aspx.* Why not contact us to see how we could help you and your organisation?

Newsletter

IT governance is one of the hottest topics in business today, not least because it is also the fastest moving, so what better way to keep up than by subscribing to ITG's free monthly newsletter *Sentinel?* It provides monthly updates and resources across the whole spectrum of IT governance subject matter, including risk management, information security, ITIL and IT service management, project governance, compliance and so much more. Subscribe for your free copy at:

www.itgovernance.co.uk/newsletter.aspx.

EU for product safety is Stephen Evans, The Mill Enterprise Hub, Stagreenan, Drogheda, Co. Louth, A92 CD3D, Ireland. (servicecentre@itgovernance.eu)

www.ingramcontent.com/pod-product-compliance
Lightning Source LLC
Chambersburg PA
CBHW071552080326
40690CB00056B/1799

* 9 7 8 1 8 4 9 2 8 0 2 9 7 *